The Reconciliation of a Penitent:
Form One

C000055938

Church House Publishing

Published by   Church House Publishing
                    Church House
                    Great Smith Street
                    London SW1P 3AZ

Copyright ©   *The Archbishops' Council 2006*

                    First published 2006
                    Second impression 2010

ISBN   978 0 7151 2177 1

Printed and bound by Core Publications Ltd.

Typeset in Gill Sans by John Morgan studio
Designed by John Morgan studio

The material in this booklet is extracted from
Common Worship: Christian Initiation. It comprises:

¶   The Reconciliation of a Penitent: Form One
¶   Authorized Absolutions

Pagination   This booklet has two sets of page numbers. The outer numbers are
              the booklet's own page numbers, while the inner numbers near the
              centre of most pages refer to the equivalent pages in *Common
              Worship: Christian Initiation.*

¶ Authorization

The Reconciliation of a Penitent: Form One has been commended by the House of Bishops of the General Synod for use by priests in exercise of their discretion under Canon B 5 of the Canons of the Church of England.

Authorized Absolution 1 is taken from *The Book of Common Prayer* with minor variations. Use of it in this form falls within the discretion canonically allowed to the minister under Canon B 5.

The Reconciliation of a Penitent

¶ *Introductory Note*

This order may be appropriately used when a person's conscience is burdened with a particular sin, when a person wishes to make a new beginning in the Christian life, or as part of a regular personal discipline.

The Book of Common Prayer includes the following pastoral exhortation: '… if there be any of you, who by this means [self-examination, confession and repentance] cannot quiet his own conscience herein, but requireth further comfort or counsel, let him come to me, or to some other discreet and learned Minister of God's Word, and open his grief, that by the ministry of God's holy Word he may receive the benefit of absolution, together with ghostly counsel and advice, to the quieting of his conscience, and avoiding of all scruple and doubtfulness.'

The aim of such a ministry of comfort and counsel is to establish an individual in the freedom and forgiveness of Christ. It can be exercised in a variety of ways at the discretion of the minister. The provision of these two orders is not intended to limit such discretion.

The reconciliation of a penitent, even when celebrated privately, remains a corporate action of the Church, because sin affects the unity of the body; through the absolution the penitent is restored to full fellowship in Christ. In *Common Worship: Christian Initiation* two forms of the rite are provided. This booklet contains the first form, which is the simpler form. It follows the traditional pattern of the western Church. The second form is an individual renewal of the baptismal covenant and may be used in situations where someone has been separated from the Church's fellowship because of sin or personal circumstances.

¶ *Explanatory Guidelines*

Preparation

The priest and penitent should prepare themselves carefully for this ministry. This includes both the desire for the illuminating presence of the Holy Spirit and the willingness to examine self in the light of God's commandments and the example of Christ.

The Greeting

The priest welcomes the penitent warmly and gives any necessary explanatory help to enable the penitent to participate fully in the rite.

Readings

In Form 1, the priest uses one or more short readings to encourage the penitent to recognize his or her sins in the light of God's word and to have confidence in his mercy. The reading of verses from Psalm 51 enables priest and penitent to acknowledge their common sinfulness and need of God's forgiveness. Where appropriate, the penitent may be invited to read a passage from the Bible.

Confession and Counsel

The confession of sins may be made in the penitent's own words, or using the forms provided with the optional insertion of particular named sins. The priest should give whatever help may be required to enable the penitent to articulate those sins for which absolution is desired. Such help will often be given before the liturgical rite is celebrated as part of an extended pastoral conversation; however, where circumstances dictate, this may take place within the rite. Sometimes, in the light of such counsel, particular issues may be clarified and motives examined; the role of the priest is to enable the penitent to make confession with integrity. This underlies the reference in the rubric to assisting the penitent 'to complete' his or her confession. The priest should seek to enable the penitent to recognize the reality of human frailty and God's all-embracing mercy and grace.

After confession, the priest may, with the goodwill of the penitent, offer counsel or advice.

The rubric referring to restitution is related to the desire for amendment of life. In some cases, a particular course of action will recommend itself – just as, in the Gospel tradition, Zacchaeus makes restitution to those he had defrauded (Luke 19.8). In other cases, this may be a willingness to seek practical reconciliation with others. This leads naturally into the Act of Contrition.

The priest may recommend some prayer or action as a sign of repentance, thanksgiving, and growth in discipleship. This may include Bible reading or other devotional reading, almsgiving, or the renewal of a personal rule of life. Prayer texts such as the Lord's Prayer, the 'Jesus Prayer' or other well-known devotional prayers are often recommended. It should always be stressed that the role of such penances is to assist the penitent in walking in newness of life; it is not about 'earning forgiveness' or being 'punished'.

In some circumstances and in some traditions of the Church, there may be a discernment that the ministry of personal prayer is a natural response to confession and counsel before absolution is pronounced. Such prayer ministry may be accompanied by the laying on of hands and/or anointing with the oil of healing. Where this ministry is unfamiliar to the penitent, care should be taken in explaining its function and form. While the rite suggests that such ministry precedes absolution, nevertheless, there may be circumstances, at the discretion of the priest, where it may follow the Absolution.

Act of Contrition

The act or prayer of contrition arises from the desire, as expressed in the Collect for Ash Wednesday, that God should create and make in us new and contrite hearts. The act of contrition expresses the desire and intention before God to turn away from sin and to walk in newness of life. The penitent may use his or her own words or the form provided.

Absolution

The priest lays hands on the penitent, or extends hands over the penitent. The priest may make the sign of the cross over the penitent, or on the penitent's forehead, recalling the baptismal liturgy. The priest uses an authorized form of absolution.

Thanksgiving

The priest and penitent may make an act of thanksgiving, followed by a prayer which celebrates the reconciliation of the penitent to God and to the Church. The Lord's Prayer may be said.

The Dismissal

The priest may bless the penitent before the formal dismissal.

Notes

Confidentiality

The ministry of reconciliation requires that what is said in confession to a priest may not be disclosed, as is set out more fully in the *Guidelines for the Professional Conduct of the Clergy* approved by the Convocations of Canterbury and York in 2003:

7   Call their hearers to repentance

In Christ's name absolve, and declare forgiveness of sins

7.1   The ministry of reconciliation, as an extension of Jesus' own ministry, lies at the heart of this vocation. It is to be exercised gently, patiently and undergirded by mutual trust.

7.2   There can be no disclosure of what is confessed to a priest. This principle holds even after the death of the penitent. The priest may not refer to what has been learnt in confession, even to the penitent, unless explicitly permitted. Some appropriate action of contrition and reparation may be required before absolution is given. A priest may withhold absolution.

7.3   Where abuse of children or vulnerable adults is admitted in the context of confession, the priest should urge the person to report his or her behaviour to the police or social services, and should also make this a condition of absolution, or withhold absolution until this evidence of repentance has been demonstrated.

7.4   If a penitent's behaviour gravely threatens his or her well-being or that of others, the priest, while advising action on the penitent's part, must still keep the confidence.

Note   *An appeal to the tradition of the Church demonstrates this understanding of the 'seal of the confessional' and the relevant provision in the Canons of 1604 (Canon 113) was left unrepealed by the Canons of 1969, which superseded the earlier Canons in almost every other respect. Whether the civil courts will always respect this principle of absolute confidentiality remains uncertain.*

2   Training
     Except in emergencies, this ministry should only be exercised after
     training. Any directions issued by the bishop should be followed.

3   Pastoral Circumstances
     In cases of pastoral necessity or emergency, only the confession,
     an expression of contrition and the absolution are mandatory. Other
     parts of the rite may be used by the penitent privately according to
     opportunity.

4   Confession and Counsel
     As on many occasions the priest and penitent will have had an
     extended conversation before the actual liturgical rite, the amount of
     counsel given within the rite will probably be small.

5   Restitution and tokens of repentance
     In giving advice to the penitent, the priest should encourage
     restitution where this is appropriate and may recommend some
     prayer or action as a token of repentance.

6   Ministry of Prayer, Laying on of Hands and Anointing
     Before pronouncing absolution the priest may, where appropriate,
     offer the ministry of prayer which may be accompanied by the laying
     on of hands, and may also be accompanied by anointing with the oil
     of healing. Alternatively, the anointing may be administered after the
     Absolution. When anointing is administered, the following form of
     words is used:

     'N, I anoint you in the name of God who gives you life.
     Receive Christ's forgiveness, his healing and his love.

     May the Father of our Lord Jesus Christ
     grant you the riches of his grace,
     his wholeness and his peace.'

7   Oil
     Canon B 37 provides that when anointing the priest should
     use 'pure olive oil consecrated by the bishop of the diocese or
     otherwise by the priest himself' and that the anointing should
     be made on the forehead with the sign of the cross. It may also
     be appropriate to anoint the hands. For a short form of
     Prayer over the Oil, see page 8.

A Short Form of Prayer over the Oil

Lord, holy Father, giver of health and salvation,
as your apostles anointed those who were sick and healed them,
so continue the ministry of healing in your Church.
Sanctify this oil, that those who are anointed with it
may be freed from suffering and distress,
find inward peace, and know the joy of your salvation,
through your Son, our Saviour Jesus Christ.

All **Amen.**

The Reconciliation of a Penitent

Structure

Optional parts of the service are indicated by square brackets.

¶ **The Gathering**
The Greeting
[Introduction]

¶ **The Liturgy of the Word**
Readings

¶ **Confession and Counsel**
Confession
[Giving of Counsel]
[The ministry of prayer and/or anointing]

¶ **Reconciliation**
Act of Contrition
Absolution
[Thanksgiving]
[The Lord's Prayer]

¶ **The Dismissal**
[Blessing]
The Dismissal

The Reconciliation of a Penitent: Form One

¶ *The Gathering*

The Greeting

The priest may say

In the name of the Father,
and of the Son,
and of the Holy Spirit.
Amen.

The priest welcomes the penitent, saying

The Lord Jesus, who came to reconcile sinners,
welcomes all who are penitent.
Grace, mercy and peace be with you
and also with you.

¶ The Liturgy of the Word

Readings

The priest may say

The Lord our God is gracious and merciful; he does not desire the death of sinners but rather that they should turn from their sins and live. He has given power and commandment to his ministers, to declare and pronounce to his penitent people the absolution and remission of their sins. He pardons and absolves all those who truly repent and believe in his holy gospel. Let us therefore pray that he will grant you true repentance and the grace and comfort of the Holy Spirit.

(or)

If we say that we have no sin, we deceive ourselves, and the truth is not in us. If we confess our sins, God is faithful and just to forgive us our sins and to cleanse us from all unrighteousness.   *I John 1.8,9*

The priest and penitent say together

**Have mercy on me, O God, in your great goodness;
according to the abundance of your compassion
    blot out my offences.
Wash me thoroughly from my wickedness
and cleanse me from my sin.
Make me a clean heart, O God,
and renew a right spirit within me.**   *Psalm 51.1,2,11*

Other suitable verses from Scripture may be said

Matthew 6.14,15; Matthew 11.28; Mark 1.14,15; Luke 6.31-38;
Luke 15.1-7; John 3.16; John 10.19-23; Romans 5.6-9; 8.1-2;
Romans 8.38,39; Ephesians 5.1,2; Colossians 1.12-14;
Colossians 3.8-10,12-17; I Timothy 1.15; I John 1.6,7,9; 2.1,2.

¶ Confession and Counsel

The priest says

The Lord be in your heart and on your lips
that you may truly and humbly confess your sins.

Confession

The penitent makes confession of sins in his or her own words, beginning

I confess to almighty God,
before the whole company of heaven and before you ...

or this form may be used

Almighty God,
long-suffering and of great goodness:
I confess to you,
I confess with my whole heart
my neglect and forgetfulness of your commandments,
my wrong doing, thinking, and speaking;
the hurts I have done to others,
and the good I have left undone.
In particular I confess [since my last confession in ... /
in this my first confession] ...
O God, for these, and all other sins that I cannot now remember,
I ask your forgiveness.
Forgive me, for I have sinned against you;
and raise me to newness of life;
through Jesus Christ our Lord.
Amen.

The priest may give appropriate counsel or guidance and whatever help
is necessary to enable the penitent to complete his or her confession.
The priest encourages the penitent to make restitution, and may
recommend some prayer or action as a sign of repentance.

The priest may, where appropriate, offer the ministry of prayer
(see Note 6, page 7).

¶ *Reconciliation*

Act of Contrition

The penitent makes an act of contrition using these or similar words

**My God, for love of you
I desire to hate and forsake all sins
by which I have ever displeased you;
and I resolve by the help of your grace
to commit them no more;
and to avoid all opportunities of sin.
Help me to do this,
through Jesus Christ our Lord.
Amen.**

Absolution

*The priest lays hands on, or extends hands over, the penitent. The
priest may make the sign of the cross over the penitent or on the
penitent's forehead. The priest pronounces an authorized Absolution
(pages 17–18).*

Thanksgiving

The priest and penitent may give thanks

Know that there is joy in heaven over each one who repents.

Give thanks to the Lord, for he is gracious,
for his faithfulness endures for ever.
For as the heavens are high above the earth,
so great is his mercy upon those who fear him.
As far as the east is from the west,
so far has he set our sins from us.   *Psalm 106.1; 103.11,12*

The priest may say

Merciful Lord,
we thank you that you have delivered this your servant
    from the power of sin
and restored *him/her* to your peace
in the fellowship of your Church;
strengthen *him/her* by your Spirit,
that *he/she* may please you
until *he/she* comes to the fullness of your eternal kingdom;
through Jesus Christ our Lord.
Amen.

God of grace and life,
in your love you have given us a place among your people;
keep us faithful to our baptism,
and prepare us for that glorious day
when the whole creation will be made perfect
in your Son our Saviour Jesus Christ.
Amen.

The Lord's Prayer

The priest and penitent may say the Lord's Prayer.

Our Father in heaven,
hallowed be your name,
your kingdom come,
your will be done,
on earth as in heaven.
Give us today our daily bread.
Forgive us our sins
as we forgive those who sin against us.
Lead us not into temptation
but deliver us from evil.
For the kingdom, the power,
and the glory are yours
now and for ever.
Amen.

(or)

Our Father, who art in heaven,
hallowed be thy name;
thy kingdom come;
thy will be done;
on earth as it is in heaven.
Give us this day our daily bread.
And forgive us our trespasses,
as we forgive those who trespass against us.
And lead us not into temptation;
but deliver us from evil.
For thine is the kingdom,
the power and the glory,
for ever and ever.
Amen.

¶ *The Dismissal*

The priest may say a blessing

May Christ,
who out of defeat brings new hope and a new future,
fill you with his new life;
and the blessing of God almighty,
the Father, the Son, and the Holy Spirit,
be upon you and remain with you always.
Amen.

(*or*)

May God,
who in Christ has reconciled all things in heaven and earth,
grant you grace to walk the path of forgiveness;
and the blessing of God almighty,
the Father, the Son, and the Holy Spirit,
be upon you and remain with you always.
Amen.

The Dismissal

Priest	The Lord has put away your sins.
Penitent	**Thanks be to God.**
Priest	Go in peace, and pray for me, a sinner.

¶ Authorized Absolutions

1

Our Lord Jesus Christ,
who has left power to his Church to absolve all sinners
    who truly repent and believe in him,
of his great mercy forgive you your offences:
and by his authority committed to me,
I absolve you from all your sins,
in the name of the Father,
and of the Son, and of the Holy Spirit.
Amen.

2

God, the Father of mercies,
has reconciled the world to himself
through the death and resurrection of his Son, Jesus Christ,
not counting our trespasses against us,
but sending his Holy Spirit
to shed abroad his love among us.
By the ministry of reconciliation
entrusted by Christ to his Church,
receive his pardon and peace
to stand before him in his strength alone,
this day and evermore.
Amen.

3

Almighty God, our heavenly Father,
who in his great mercy
has promised forgiveness of sins
to all those who with heartfelt repentance and true faith
    turn to him:
have mercy on you,
pardon and deliver you from all your sins,
confirm and strengthen you in all goodness,
and bring you to everlasting life,
through Jesus Christ our Lord.
Amen.

4

Almighty God,
who forgives all who truly repent,
have mercy upon you,
pardon and deliver you from all your sins,
confirm and strengthen you in all goodness,
and keep you in life eternal;
through Jesus Christ our Lord.
Amen.

5

The Lord enrich you with his grace,
and nourish you with his blessing;
the Lord defend you in trouble and keep you from all evil;
the Lord accept your prayers,
and absolve you from your offences,
for the sake of Jesus Christ, our Saviour.
Amen.

6

The almighty and merciful Lord
grant you pardon and forgiveness of all your sins,
time for amendment of life,
and the grace and strength of the Holy Spirit.
Amen.

Copyright Information

The Archbishops' Council of the Church of England and the other copyright owners and administrators of texts included in *Common Worship: Christian Initiation* have given permission for the use of their material in local reproductions on a non-commercial basis which comply with the conditions for reproductions for local use set out in the Archbishops' Council's booklet, *A Brief Guide to Liturgical Copyright*. This is available from:

www.commonworship.com

A reproduction which meets the conditions stated in that booklet may be made without an application for copyright permission or payment of a fee, but the following copyright acknowledgement must be included:

> *Common Worship: Christian Initiation*, material from which is included in this service, is copyright © The Archbishops' Council 2006.

Permission must be obtained in advance for any reproduction which does not comply with the conditions set out in *A Brief Guide to Liturgical Copyright*. Applications for permission should be addressed to:

The Copyright Administrator
The Archbishops' Council
Church House
Great Smith Street
London SW1P 3AZ
Email: copyright@c-of-e.org.uk